The Great Family Reunion

by James R. Sanderson
illustrated by Valeria Cis

Harcourt
SCHOOL PUBLISHERS

Printed in China

ISBN 10: 0-15-350139-1
ISBN 13: 978-0-15-350139-5

Ordering Options
ISBN 10: 0-15-349939-7 (Grade 4 ELL Collection)
ISBN 13: 978-0-15-349939-5 (Grade 4 ELL Collection)
ISBN 10: 0-15-357273-6 (package of 5)
ISBN 13: 978-0-15-357273-9 (package of 5)

1 2 3 4 5 6 7 8 9 10 985 12 11 10 09 08 07 06

Paula Greco organizes her family reunion. A family reunion is when many family members get together. Aunts and uncles go to reunions. Sisters and brothers go, too. So do grandparents and cousins. Family reunions are often held at a park. The family members eat food. They also play games. Most of all, they visit with one another.

Each year Paula plans her family reunion. She decides when the reunion will take place. She decides where it will be.

In January, Paula looked at the calendar.
She thought about when to have the reunion.
She decided it would be on Saturday, July 19th.

"Will you have it at the same park as last
year?" her husband, Don, asked.

"Yes, it's a good park," said Paula. "Everyone
liked it last year."

First, Paula went to the village hall. She got a
park permit. That allows her family to use a picnic
area in the park for the reunion. Next, Paula made
invitations. The invitations told when and where
the reunion would be. Finally, Paula and Don
mailed the invitations out to family members.

Paula and Don went shopping the day before the reunion. They bought food and drinks to be served at the reunion. Then Paula cleaned out the coolers. Coolers are large containers that keep food and drinks cold. The food and drinks will be in the coolers at the reunion.

Don took out the volleyball net and ball. He made sure they were in good shape. Many family members enjoyed playing volleyball at the reunions.

Paula and Don went to the park on the morning of the reunion. They set up the volleyball net and coolers. The picnic area had a pavilion, which is a building with a roof but no walls. People could also go there to get out of the rain or hot July sun.

Paula and Don took out the special T-shirts they had ordered. Each person at the reunion would get a T-shirt. The T-shirts said, "Greco Family Reunion." The T-shirts also had a picture of people laughing and eating because people at the reunion eat and laugh a lot. Paula was pleased with how the T-shirts looked.

Family members began to arrive at the park at around noon. Paula's parents walked up to the pavilion, carrying a cooler of food. Paula's Aunt Mary and Uncle Ernie arrived a few minutes later. Her cousin Carla walked up to the pavilion carrying her new baby, Stevie, in her arms. "Oh, he is so *cute!*" Paula said.

More and more family members arrived. They said hello, smiled, and hugged one another. People were glad to be together. Many of the family members only see each other once a year at the reunion.

"Here, put on your shirt," Paula said to her brother, Vince. Vince looked at the shirt.

"Hey, I like it!" he said, and he put it on. Paula and Don continued to pass out the shirts.

Family members placed their coolers and baskets on picnic tables in the pavilion. Then they visited with their relatives.

Aunt Lena and her sister, Aunt Faye, sat at a picnic table and had a nice conversation. They asked each other what they had been doing lately. They talked about their children. They talked about things they did when they were young. The two sisters laughed a lot.

"Geno, will you get me a bottle of juice, please?" Aunt Lena asked her nephew who was nearby. He walked to the cooler and returned with the bottle. "Thank you, darling," Aunt Lena said, then continued her conversation.

By 1:30 P.M., there were more than a hundred people at the reunion. Paula and her cousin Harry moved three picnic tables together to form one long table. Then Paula asked everyone to place their food on the table. People brought chicken, pasta, and vegetables. People helped themselves to food, and then they sat at the other tables to eat.

"As usual, everything is delicious!" said Grandma Greco.

It was about 2:30 P.M. by the time people finished eating. They cleaned up. Then they did the things that they enjoy. Some of the teenagers started a volleyball game. Uncle Mike placed his lawn chair just off to the side of the net. "I'm the scorekeeper," he said to the players. Some of the adults watched the game. Many of the children went to play at the playground.

Later, it was time to have the water balloon toss. One person tossed a water balloon to a teammate who tried to catch it. Often the balloon broke, and the person got all wet. This was always really funny. Pairs of teammates took turns throwing their balloons. Vince's balloon broke right on top of his head! Paula's twin cousins, Pat and Joanna, won the event.

The last big event of the reunion was the group photograph. Each year, Don took a photo of all the people at the reunion. Paula and Don helped get everyone organized in front of the pavilion. Grandma Greco sat in a chair at the very front of the group. Don set up the camera and yelled, "Say cheese!" Then he took the photo. Paula would later send copies of the photograph to all of her relatives.

People began to pack their belongings and leave as the sun went down. Relatives hugged and kissed each other and said good-bye. "I'll see you next year!" many of them said.

The reunion had been wonderful. The weather was good. Everyone came, and they all had a good time. Paula and Don finished cleaning up the picnic area. It was a lot of work to run the reunion, but Paula loved to do it. She loved her family very much.

Scaffolded Language Development

PUNCTUATION IN DIALOGUE Review punctuation marks in dialogue with students by pointing out examples in the book. Model for students how to punctuate this sentence by first writing and reading it without punctuation and then adding the punctuation marks: *"Be sure to invite cousins Rita, Nathan, and John,"* *Paula said.* Then write the following sentences on the board without punctuation, and have students approach the board to fill in the blanks. Have students chorally read each sentence after it has been punctuated.

1. The cousins organized games of volleyball badminton and baseball Aunt Lena said
2. When will the next reunion be Aunt Lena asked
3. It will be the same week next year Paula replied

 ## Language Arts

Write Key Sentences Have students write three sentences that describe things that Paula did before, during, and after the reunion.

School-Home Connection
Share Some Memories Tell students to share this story with family members. Have them discuss some family gatherings that they have attended. Encourage them to share some of the words in this story with family members.

Word Count: 960